ACCOMPANIMENTS FOR DOUBLE BA

arranged by Jill and Keith Hartley

TORTUES
Le Carnaval des Animaux

Book 1 No.2

CAMILLE SAINT-SAËNS
(1835—1921)

Reproduced by permission of Editions Durand S. A., Paris/United Music Publishers Ltd.

THE MERRY PEASANT

Album for the Young (Op.68)

Book 1 No.5

ROBERT SCHUMANN
(1810—56)

ENTR'ACTE

Incidental Music to 'Rosamunde'

Book 1 No.6

FRANZ SCHUBERT
(1797—1828)

PILGRIMS' MARCH

Symphony 4 'The Italian'

Book 1 No.9

Andante con moto

FELIX MENDELSSOHN
(1809—47)

MINUET
Aires and Dances

Book 1 No.11

JOHN ECCLES
(1660—1735)

NOW IS THE MONTH OF MAYING

Book 1 No.16

THOMAS MORLEY
(1557—1603)

MARCH

Judas Maccabaeus

Book 1 No.15

GEORGE FRIDERIC HANDEI
(1685—1759)

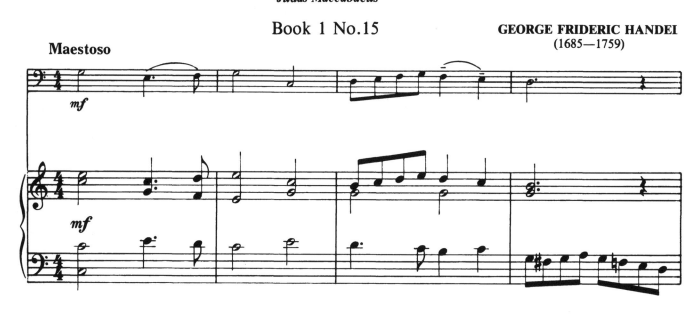

OLD FRENCH SONG

Album for the Young

Book 1 No.17

PYOTR TCHAIKOVSKY
(1840—93)

MY HEART EVER FAITHFUL

Cantata 68

Book 1 No.21

JOHANN SEBASTIAN BACH
(1685—1750)

ANDANTINO
Symphony 4

Book 1 No.24

PYOTR TCHAIKOVSKY
(1840—93)

MARCH

Scipio

Book 1 No.23

GEORGE FRIDERIC HANDEL
(1685—1759)

ANDANTE
Variation 6: Rococo Variations (Op.33)

Book 1 No.25

PYOTR TCHAIKOVSKY
(1840—93)

GREENSLEEVES

Book 1 No.30

Trad. English

JUPITER
The Planets

Book 1 No.26

GUSTAV HOLST
(1874—1934)

JESU, JOY OF MAN'S DESIRING

Cantata 147

Book 1 No.29

JOHANN SEBASTIAN BACH
(1685—1750)

ANDANTE
Trumpet Concerto
Book 1 No.32

JOSEPH HAYDN
(1732—1809)

Cantabile

TOREADOR'S SONG

Carmen: Act 2 No.14

Book 1 No.39

GEORGES BIZET
(1838—75)

ST. ANTHONY CHORALE

Haydn Variations

Book 1 No.40

JOHANNES BRAHMS
(1833—97)

MINUET

The Anna Magdalena Notebook

Book 1 No.42

JOHANN SEBASTIAN BACH
(1685—1750)

STRING SONATA 3

Book 2 No.8

GIOACHINO ROSSINI
(1792—1868)

SYMPHONY 45

'Farewell'

Book 2 No.17

JOSEPH HAYDN
(1732—1809)

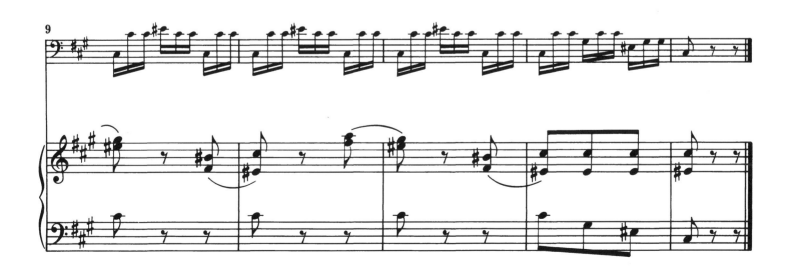

L'ÉLÉPHANT
Le Carnaval des Animaux
Book 2 No.9

CAMILLE SAINT-SAËNS
(1835—1921)

Allegretto pomposo

SYMPHONY 8
Book 2 No.13

ANTONIN DVOŘÁK
(1841—1904)

VIOLIN CONCERTO 2

Book 2 No.18

JOHANN SEBASTIAN BACH
(1685—1750)

SYMPHONY 31
'Horn Signal'
Book 2 No.26

JOSEPH HAYDN
(1732—1809)

Variation 7

RIGOLETTO ACT II
Book 2 No.29

GUISEPPE VERDI
(1813—1901)

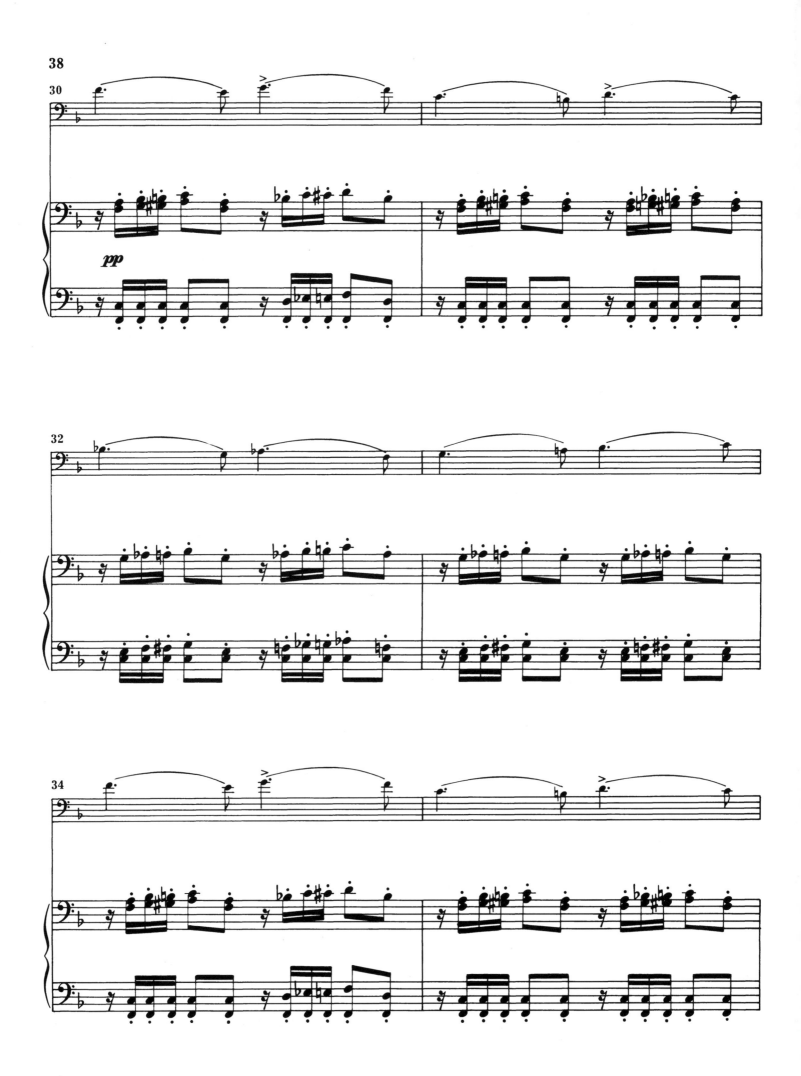

Printed and bound in Great Britain by
Caligraving Limited Thetford Norfolk